B A R S
NITECLUBS
&
TAVERNS

international interiors

B A R S
NITECLUBS
& TAVERNS

INTERIOR *details*

An Imprint of

P B C   I N T E R N A T I O N A L, I N C.

Distributor to the book trade in the United States and Canada:

Rizzoli International Publications Inc.
300 Park Avenue South
New York, NY 10010

Distributor to the art trade in the United States and Canada:

PBC International, Inc.
One School Street
Glen Cove, NY 11542
1-800-527-2826
Fax 516-676-2738

Distributor throughout the rest of the world:

Hearst Books International
1350 Avenue of the Americas
New York, NY 10019

Library of Congress Cataloging-in-Publication Data

Bars, niteclubs & taverns / the editors of PBC International,
Inc.
       p.   cm.
     Includes index.
     ISBN 0-86636-226-6
     1. Hotels, taverns, etc.--United States.   2. Architecture,
Modern--20th century--United States.   I. PBC International.
II. Title: Bars, niteclubs & taverns.
NA7852.537   1993
725'.72--dc20   93-12134
                                                                    CIP

CAVEAT—Information in this text is believed accurate, and will pose
no problem for the student or casual reader. However, the author was often
constrained by information contained in signed release forms, information
that could have been in error or not included at all. Any misinformation
(or lack of information) is the result of failure in these attestations.
The author has done whatever is possible to insure accuracy.

Typography by
TypeLink, Inc.

Printed in China

10 9 8 7 6 5 4 3 2 1

Table of Contents

Introduction

TV news drones in the background, too bright morning light intrudes, the caffeine kicks in, images of accelerated change and sudden disintegration struggle into focus from the newspaper; an unpredictable pluralism bursts through the rust of the once bisecting iron curtain and implodes in places; another fossil fuel fed factory belches, dies, and fertilizes the growth of a silicon chip labor or fiber optic plant, which in turn lubricates ever faster cycles of reinvention in a culture which celebrates its heterogeneity and lack of use for the comforts of tradition.

In the homogenized synthetic office cubicle, midmorning tension builds as a bombardment of data flows in amidst the nervous hum of phones, faxes and fluorescent lights.

A midday breeze sulks through the city, harasses tortuously manicured plants, spins the revolving doors of arrogant and punitive reductive structures.

By twilight, at the end of a workday of cautious confrontation, calculation and overstimulation, spiritual enervation prevails.

In the nighttime, a need for emotional sustenance ripens, a need for refuge from the facts of daytime.

Even the door handle at the threshold of escape foreshadows the unquantifiable architecture of the room beyond, a structure built on the logic of improvised jazz or a dream.

The vestibule compresses, warm and worn, whispers something vaguely familiar, the déjà vu of a long forgotten Hollywood image. Perhaps a whiff of once upon a time mingles with a hint of tomorrow, filling the room, which murmurs in a viscous, rhythmic visual dialect punctuated by amber light and the possibility of romance or violence.

The architecture inhales at the peak of a riff, the colors fade, humanity nudges toward intimate eddies of conversation, then toward the whirlpool of dance. A sense of community and humor presides, mitigating the predatory overtones of assembly in the night.

—Jordan Mozer

Avant-garde designer Jordan Mozer of Jordan Mozer & Associates, Chicago, Illinois, was the visionary behind the Tempest and Cairo 720 nightspots included in this volume. He is currently designing Stars, a space-fantasy restaurant to be located in Frankfurt, Germany.

Dance Clubs,
Discos, Niteclubs,
Entertainment Spots

BACCHUS
New York, New York

By contrasting design recalling the simple and pastoral charms of rural Tuscany with a stark, industrial look, a space of immense visual excitement was created for this New York restaurant and nightclub. The central dining area overflows with details reminiscent of the Italian countryside such as Corinthian columns faux-finished in a Tuscan hue, an exposed brick wall with arched, flower-filled niches, and alabaster pendant fixtures. Simple, natural-toned farmhouse chairs and bar-stools, and a raised, carpeted area furnished with wicker seating add to the sense of warmth and bucolic charm. An expansive, jiggered steel and copper bar, backed by an arcing steel slab with square cutouts and wood shelving, adds a modern, though appropriate touch. A wooden arbor supports faux versions of the grape vines Bacchus' namesake was famous for.

The industrial look of the bar and dance area of the space offers a startling visual contrast to the warmth of the dining area. The angular, metal-topped bar is faced with undulating fiberglass panels covered by wire meshing and back-lit with iridescent colors. The unadorned floor and white, oversized cylindrical columns add to the minimalist appearance of the space.

CLIENT: MLRR Entertainment Corp. DESIGN TEAM: Michael David Berzak, Principal; Richard J. Kahn, Project Designer DESIGN FIRM: Michael David Berzak Architecture SQUARE FOOTAGE: 15,000 BUDGET: $1.25 million PHOTOGRAPHY: Photography by Lars Lönninge

Photography by Lars Lönninge

Photography by Lars Lönninge

BIG HAUS
New York, New York

Celebrating the Bauhaus artistic movement of Germany, New York City's Big Haus is filled with the industrial look and artifacts of that era. Most striking is the chandelier designed by Robert Singer. Its light fixtures terminate tentacle-like goose-neck tubing sections that twist grotesquely. In the smoky atmosphere of the bar, spears of light shoot from these fixtures in random directions, creating unusual effects. Light also pours eerily from the registers of what used to be a ventilator duct. Large, blocky, sans-serif lettering in the mural on the long wall recalls the Bauhaus school, as do the custom wall sconces, the bar constructed of black leather and mahogany and the leather and faux-pony furniture.

As a counterpoint to the Bauhaus theme, the combination of light/dark finishes and contrasts in lighting also suggest Biedermeier-type design. Theatrical lighting and unusual wood accents, including curtain-shaped pieces that frame a glass block wall, also present a stage-like atmosphere for this dramatic and singular club.

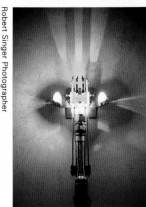

Robert Singer Photographer

CLIENT: Kurt Von Schlosberg, Marc Cosnard DESIGN TEAM: Jane Millet, Interior Design; Robert Singer, Lighting Consultant DESIGN FIRM: Robert Singer & Assoc., Inc. SQUARE FOOTAGE: 2,500 BUDGET: $10,000 (lighting)
PHOTOGRAPHER: Robert Singer

CAIRO 720
Chicago, Illinois

Nightclub and bistro Cairo 720 brings a timeless collage of Jordan Mozer's Egyptian ideas, whims and obsessions to the Chicago area. Ancient Egypt is apparent in the elegant, stylized upstairs, with its mosaic spiral floor rendered in black and lapis lazuli blue granite, cracked walls oxidized with ammonium nitrate, and a bar fashioned after the hieroglyphical symbol for water. The colors used in the finishes were sacred to the ancient Egyptians as well, green symbolizing the rebirth of the Nile, yellow as the color of the sand and earth, and gold as the color of the sun. Rusted, cast iron Victorian Corinthian columns recall the English colonization period of Egypt. The circular forms used in the back bar's cognac "sarcophagus" cabinet, the use of bird's eye maple, and the circular mirrors and the bar stools, specially designed for the project are reminiscent of the Egypt-inspired French Art Deco period.

The club is also split in accordance with ancient Egyptian mythology. While the upper, vibrant level represents the land of the living, on this side of the Nile, the stark lower level, with its exposed brick and beams and its scarcity of decoration represents the land of the dead.

CLIENT: **Jerry Kleiner** DESIGN TEAM: **Jordan Mozer, Paul Orzeske, Nadine Reed-Royal, Danny Taylor** DESIGN FIRM: **Jordan Mozer and Associates, Limited** SQUARE FOOTAGE: **5,500** BUDGET: **$605,000** PHOTOGRAPHER: Daniel Bakke Photography

CLUB ZEI
Washington, District of Columbia

The Zei is a four-story night-club within an industrial building that formerly housed an electrical power sub-station in downtown Washington D.C. The club's concept drew directly from the industrial style of the building, with new architectural components inserted as counterpoints. Thus a theatrical experience is created, where the architectural elements serve as the dominant characters, each with a distinct personality and function.

The plan is organized around four major components: the Cone, the Solid Wall, the Grid Wall and the Video Wall. The Cone represents what was formerly the smokestack of the power plant; it serves as the point of entry and displays the immensity of the space. Emanating out of the Cone are the Grid Wall, with its large, sheet metal-clad mirrors, emphasizing the spectacle of the people and frame the bar area, and the Solid Wall, containing the lounge area and exhibits the voyeuristic aspect of the nightclub experience. To introduce the fourth character, perhaps the most interesting aspect of the club, a rusted sheet metal curtain was draped to one side, exposing a 30-foot-high wall of videos. The contrast of the state-of-the-art technology with the decay of corroded metal creates a compelling dialog between old and new. Color and dramatic lighting, used effectively as a foil to the light wood and monochromatic nature of the building help create an atmosphere of excitement and drama irresistible to dancing patrons.

CLIENT: Paul Cohn DESIGN TEAM: Olvia Demetriou, Principal/Project Architect; Theodore Adamstein, Brian O'Connell, Bill Bourque, Lori Arrasmith, Staff Architects DESIGN FIRM: Adamstein & Demetriou SQUARE FOOTAGE: 11,000 BUDGET: $1,450,000 PHOTOGRAPHER: Jerome Adamstein

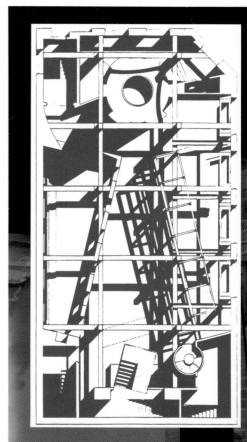

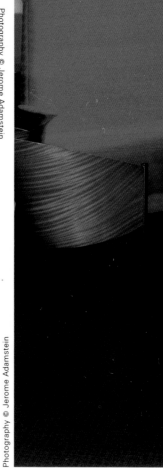

Photography © Jerome Adamstein

HEAVEN

Pittsburgh, Pennsylvania

The vast spaces of the discotheque and nightclub Heaven and the four-star restaurant Les Nuages (The Clouds) are linked both architecturally and thematically in this Pittsburgh site by Bromley Caldari Architects. Heaven is dominated by a fish scale stained glass dome (circa 1910) that is backlit by German Opera Lights. Circling the dome are aircraft landing lights in banks of four colors that can be chased and zoned. The main and side bars are lit by double bands of neon that follow the groins of the vaulted ceilings. The Gold Room, at the top of the grand marble staircase that fronts the dance floor, contains a bar accented by gelled fluorescent tubes visible under the front counter behind the three quarter inch reveal.

The two-story cocktail/ waiting lounge of Les Nuages features a wine selection displayed on industrial wire shelving, modular seating and moveable bar stools. Open stairs with original iron railing leads to the dining area one flight up, where the original turn of the century dentil moldings, ceiling, and architectural details are visible. The restaurant has an open, yet intimate atmosphere that was achieved by dividing the restaurant into three sections with brushed aluminum blinds and industrial pipe railings.

© Jaime Ardiles-Arce

CLIENT: **Stern Entertainment Systems, Inc.** DESIGN TEAM: **R. Scott Bromley, Jerry Caldari, Robin Jacobsen, Stan Fedenick, Fern Mallis** DESIGN FIRM: **Bromley Caldari Architects** SQUARE FOOTAGE: **N/A** BUDGET: **N/A** PHOTOGRAPHER: **Jaime Ardiles-Arce**

HORIZONS

Toronto, Ontario

Celebrated as the highest nightclub in the world, Horizons, located in the CN Tower in Toronto, was specifically redesigned around two major criteria: to highlight the remarkable 360-degree view the site offers, and to work with and accentuate the semi-circular shape the bar is based on. Stretching around the club's 180-degree perimeter are a series of curved, raised platforms that afford panoramic views of the city and lake. Paralleling this perimeter is an impressive, fifty foot, wood and stainless steel-clad bar. Polished steel is also used liberally in the railings, chair backs and pillars, offsetting the hardwood dance area.

The floor-to-ceiling windows that circle the club reflect the two illuminated feature sculptures and the broad striped central floor lamp. The custom, leather-upholstered bench seating provides both a solid mass and an oasis to balance the feeling of height emphasized by the other planning and design features.

CLIENT: **CN Tower/La Tour CN** DESIGN TEAM: **Martin Hirschberg, Principal; Robert Graham, Project Leader, Senior Designer; Susan Lum, Project Coordinator; John Radchenko, Food Facility Planner; Sarah Withey, Designer** DESIGN FIRM: **Hirschberg Design Group Inc.** SQUARE FOOTAGE: **10,000** BUDGET: **$1.15 million** PHOTOGRAPHER: **Christopher Dew Productions Photography/Christopher Dew, Robert Johnston**

Christopher Dew Productions Photography/Christopher Dew, Robert Johnston

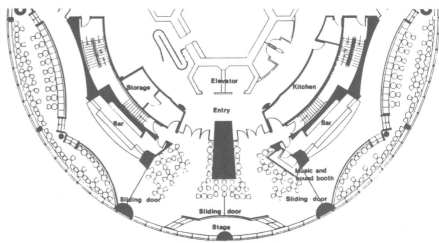

KRYSTAL'S

Melville, New York

The site for Krystal's of Long Island, which housed a three room restaurant, was completely gutted and opened up to make room for this versatile and dynamic nightclub. Jagged-edged stone is the central element around which Krystal's was designed, and can be found in many incarnations throughout the club. For example, two bars which flank the interior are partially covered by a dark stone finish laminate over a coral-colored background. This stone extends out to create a jagged-edged pocket lit by coral-colored neon. The soffits over these bars are illuminated by the same neon to both accent and balance the space. Dramatic, jagged-edged openings opposite the dance floor, back-lit from below by purple neon, lend interest to the long solid wall and balance the room.

The structural columns were worked into the design of the room by wrapping them in a multi-colored stone finish laminate and topping them with neon. Originally a design problem, they now work as supports for the soffit above the dance floor. The expanse of black mirror on the walls is broken up by coral-colored columns that seem to support the standup counter. A lounge with a pool table adds competition and fun to the atmosphere, while a VIP sitting lounge offers a quieter conversation area for those wishing a respite from the excitement of the rest of the club.

CLIENT: Mitch Feuerstein DESIGN TEAM: Mandi QuKay, Designer; Tom Fisher, Project Director DESIGN FIRM: Mandi QuKay Design & Planning Inc. SQUARE FOOTAGE: 5,000 BUDGET: $500,000 PHOTOGRAPHER: Van Blerck Photography

LAURA BELLE
New York, New York

Elegance and style are presented in a thoroughly modern way in Laura Belle, the latest addition to New York's nighttime dining and dancing scene and site of "happenings" from Ralph Lauren's Christmas party to Madonna's "Truth or Dare" bash. A gloriously romantic, almost cinematic mood is created in this totally new supper club through the brilliant use of lighting, period decor, and innovative design.

The club is furnished in rich wood finishes and deep red upholstery, giving it a luxurious undertone. A startling exterior facade with columns and cornice washed in red and blue tints looms over the dance floor, enhancing the grandeur of the space. The spectacular seven by ten foot, owner-designed chandeliers can be lowered within ten feet of the floor if a more intimate feel is desired. General illumination is provided by wall-washers, downlights and sconces, which are completely user-controllable, in addition to candle lamps finished in silver which illuminate each table. The exclusive use of incandescent lighting provides a "lush" feel, and lighting designer Robert Singer says, "the general ambiance in the space is very, very flattering. Everyone looks great."

Joseph Coscia, Jr. Inset: Joseph Coscia, Jr.

CLIENT: Michael "Buzzy" O'Keefe DESIGN TEAM: Robert Singer, Lighting Designer; Michael "Buzzy" O'Keefe, Interior Designer; Peter Mullen, Architect DESIGN FIRM: Robert Singer & Assoc., Inc. SQUARE FOOTAGE: N/A BUDGET: N/A PHOTOGRAPHER: Joseph Coscia, Jr.

METROPOLIS

Irvine, California

By utilizing ordinary materials in unexpected ways, the Metropolis billiards club takes the public's perception of design to a new level. For example, when riveted steel is used as a trim, it is contrasted with rich wood grains. The wood paneling on the blade wall, which curves sinuously, is terminated by a welded and riveted slice of steel. Steel I-beams are centrally supported by Corinthian columns with gold leafed capitals. Gold leafing is also used provocatively in the stout, upward-tapering columns that support the atrium.

Design choices such as secluded alcoves, separate atrium level for seating customers, and violet curtains that delineate lower level areas give the Metropolis a sense of intimacy. Dancing and billiards-playing customers, however, are pleased by the apparent abundance of space.

CLIENT: Hanour Corporation   DESIGN TEAM: Rick McCormack, Jackie Hanson   DESIGN FIRM: Hatch Design Group   SQUARE FOOTAGE: 11,149   BUDGET: $1.5 million   PHOTOGRAPHER: Ron Pollard

Ron Pollard

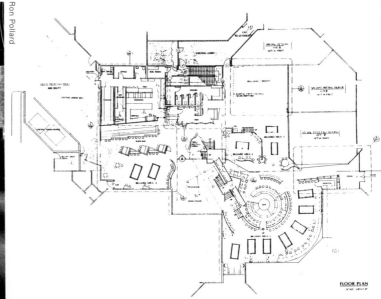

FLOOR PLAN

Ron Pollard

METROPOLIS ROOM
At the Shark Club
Costa Mesa, California

The Shark Club, established in 1990, is an upscale billiards hall with dining and bar facilities. While the main club would be filled to capacity, the Metropolis Room would remain empty, due to its uninviting, "stand-offish" atmosphere.

Renovations transformed the room into what is now an inviting "retro-rococo" space. The walls are draped with enormous quantities of rich upholstery fabric. A crimson mohair sofa and jewel-colored, overstuffed cushions beckon invitingly. Four Brazilian cherry platforms support tatami tables. Both the engraved hardwood of the billiard tables and the frame for the immense mirror are trimmed with ornate gold leafing. Custom-designed lights, including conical, jewel-draped overhead lamps and torch-shaped sconces complete the effect. The Metropolis Room has definitely aided the Shark Club in overcoming its conservative Orange County location and put it on the leading edge of design for Southern California.

Ron Pollard

CLIENT: Hanour Corporation DESIGN TEAM: Rick McCormack, Jackie Hanson DESIGN FIRM: Hatch Design Group SQUARE FOOTAGE: 600 BUDGET: $80,000 PHOTOGRAPHER: Ron Pollard

Ron Pollard

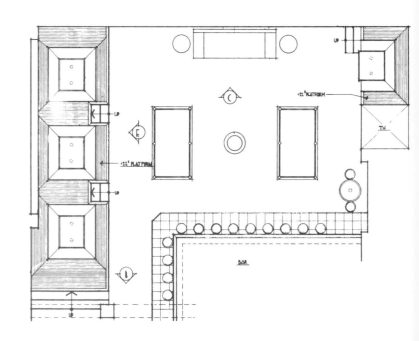

NITE LITES DANCE CLUB

Greensboro, North Carolina

Amethyst, sapphire and hot pink set the tone for this electric night spot, located in the Embassy Suites Hotel. Frequented by both hotel guests and local residents, this futuristic lounge is marked by the elaborate lighting on its walls and ceiling. Strategic placement of the lighting, in conjunction with carefully hung soffits, outlined in neon, draw attention to the centrally located dance floor.

An interesting feature of the club, furthering its contemporary mood, is the custom-made, electra-dye carpet sensitive to black light. Fiber optic art is artistically placed throughout the space, and reflected in several mirrors, imparting a more spacious feel. In a separate seating area of the club, light wood and chrome are highlighted by subdued pink lighting, offering a dramatic contrast to the black laminate drink rails and tabletops.

Jerry Blow Architectural Photography

CLIENT: John Q. Hammons Industries DESIGN TEAM: Linda Higgins, President/Co-Owner DESIGN FIRM: ONE DESIGN CENTER, Inc. SQUARE FOOTAGE: 5,000 BUDGET: $535,000 PHOTOGRAPHER: Jerry Blow, Jerry Blow Architectural Photography

ODEUM
Tokyo, Japan

This plush karaoke club was created as a retreat from the frenzy of daily life, a place where people could come to indulge in relaxation and entertainment. To create this ambiance, rich colors and soft velvet fabrics are used to inject the room with sensuality and comfort. Red, the dominant hue, is used lavishly in the luxurious carpet and high-backed, futuristic chairs.

An "other worldly" mood suffuses the club, created by voluptuous, spiral-shaped structural columns that circle the club's perimeter, and a spiral-shaped, marbleized bar that glows provocatively. This "alien" feel is enhanced by floor mounted bar stools shaped like exotic mushrooms, with pedestals echoing the look of the main columns. The lighting is subdued, and serves largely to highlight the sinuous curves found throughout the club.

CLIENT: **Jasmac Co. Ltd.** DESIGN TEAM: **Larry Totah, Designer; Noni So, Project Manager; Dan Sauerbray, Joselito Bautista Angelica Aliso Sr., Heidi Toll, Project Team** DESIGN FIRM: **Totah Design Inc.** SQUARE FOOTAGE: **7,900** BUDGET: **N/A** PHOTOGRAPHER: **Nacása & Partners Inc.**

Nacása & Partners inc. Inset: Nacása & Partners inc.

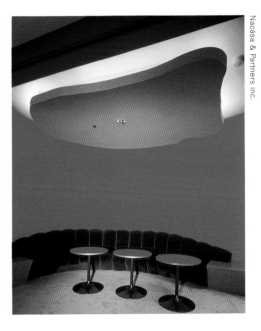

Nacása & Partners inc.

Nacása & Partners inc.

Nacása & Partners inc.

Nacása & Partners inc.

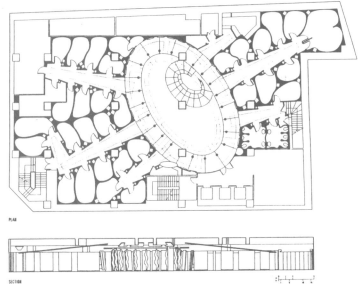

PLAN

SECTION

GRAND HYATT HONG KONG

Hong Kong

The Grand Hyatt Hong Kong is a romantic, opulent hotel where the designers strove to mix elements of both Eastern and Western cultures. A subtlety of design is played against the theatrical enormity of scale—a grand hotel in the manner of the 1930s. The lobby has a strong impact on those "making their entrance" with its dramatic, custom mosaic marble floor. In the public spaces of the Grand Hyatt, art is used to complete and reflect the intensity and grandeur of the hotel.

The bar areas are no less stunning, and entering through full-length glass doors trimmed in gold, one is overwhelmed by the elegance of the room. The same gold trim used for the doors is also repeated in the floor to ceiling mirrors surrounding the piano stage. Combined with spot lighting and a gold curtain, a dramatic counterpoint is struck against the black marble and subdued lighting of the central bar.

CLIENT: New World Development Co., Ltd. DESIGN TEAM: Alan Stephens, Director; Deborah Ballinger, Oscar Llinas, Project Decorators; Robert Bilkey, John Chan, Julius Cristobal, Project Designers; Howard Hirsch, Alan Stephens, Principals in Charge; David Carter, Design Consultant; David Ho, Assistant Project Manager; Jeff Miller, Lighting Consultant; Susan Kay, Debbie Ferrel, Art Consultants DESIGN FIRM: NG Chun Man & Associates, Architects; Hirsch/Bedner & Associates, Interior Design SQUARE FOOTAGE: N/A BUDGET: $21,000,000 (Hotel) PHOTOGRAPHER: © Jaime Ardiles-Arce

SOUNDS OF BRAZIL
New York, New York

The night scene at S.O.B.'s continues to attract diverse crowds from all over New York City. Recent renovations have helped the club keep pace with the customers' needs and prevent it from "burning out." Robin Boyer's recent tropical design elements have brought an infusion of energy and fun. Immovable columns in the middle of the club posed an initial problem. The designers chose to paint them in playful, tropical colors to resemble guava trees, to integrate them with the overall design scheme, where they serve as a proscenium arch for the stage area. A change in levels became a natural separation of the bar from the dance area and theatrical lights with colored gels were used to add drama to the diamond-patterned dance floor.

The thatch-roofed bar and multi-colored neon signage, superimposed on a bamboo wall reflect the tropical roots of the club and evoke an exotic ambiance. To further promote this feeling, neutral wood barstools were combined with woven, rush seats.

Photos by Ross Muir

CLIENT: **R. Larry Gold** DESIGN TEAM: **Larry Bogdanow, Principal; Warren Ashworth, Project Captain; Robin Boyers, Interior Design Consultant** DESIGN FIRM: **L. Bogdanow & Associates, Architects** SQUARE FOOTAGE: **4,000 plus cellar and upstairs offices** BUDGET: **$300,000** PHOTOGRAPHER: **Ross Muir**

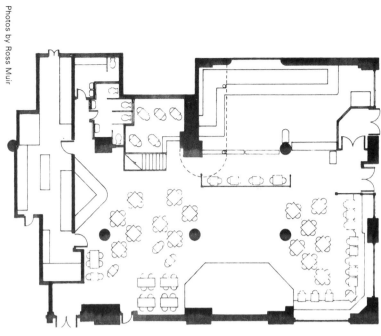

Photos by Ross Muir

SOUTH BEACH 'N THE ISLANDS
Chicago, Illinois

Attracting a young Latin American clientele, South Beach 'n the Islands is a Chicago nightclub which manages to radiate the glamour of South Miami Beach while at the same time offering a sense of the adventure of a voyage to the Caribbean Islands. This is accomplished through the division of the club into two levels, each having its own distinct decor and atmosphere. The first level, which surrounds a circular bar, emulates the glamour of modern Miami. It is dominated by scalloped furniture and art trimmed liberally with chrome and lit by blue and pink neon; the "Moon Over Miami" chandelier lends interest to the beamed ceiling.

The second level is an open space broken up into individual areas delineated by minor gingerbread screening gaily colored in the vibrant hues of traditional Caribbean homes. The "Frog Pond," with its sunken dance floor, DJ booth, and go-go stages; the "Back Room," with its brothel booths replete with oversized seating and peeling, stained floral wallpaper, and the beach and hotel bars, which serve exotic tropical drinks flow into one another yet retain their individual ambiance and sense of space.

Mark Ballogg, Steinkamp/Ballogg, Chicago

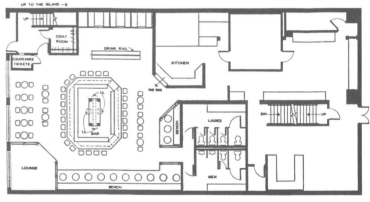

SOUTH BEACH 'N THE ISLANDS, CHICAGO ILLINOIS   "SOUTH BEACH"- FIRST LEVEL

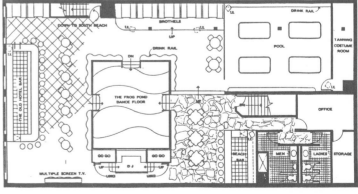

SOUTH BEACH 'N THE ISLANDS, CHICAGO ILLINOIS   THE ISLANDS - SECOND LEVEL

CLIENT: **Jose Venzor** DESIGN TEAM: **Marve H. Cooper, Designer; Tom Strobel, Artist; Shiela Strobel, Art & Decorative Effects** DESIGN FIRM: **Marve Cooper Design** SQUARE FOOTAGE: **7,000** BUDGET: **$350,000** PHOTOGRAPHY: **Mark Ballogg, Steinkamp/Ballogg, Chicago**

Mark Ballogg, Steinkamp/Ballogg, Chicago

Mark Ballogg, Steinkamp/Ballogg, Chicago

STUDIO 54

New York, New York

Creating a new theatrical experience within an old theatrical shell, Studio 54 has transformed the Gallo Opera House (built in 1927) into a glamorous, vibrant space, where contrasts between old and new only serve to heighten the excitement of the club. The club's lobby initiates this dichotomy, with striped directional carpeting passing beneath the original mirrored arches with elaborate neoclassical moldings and plaster work to a dramatic new stainless steel moveable sculpture. A nine foot high crystal chandelier from the eighteenth century is lit by four rotating laser beams.

The main dance floor, which was the original stage surface is complemented by a Flying Ceiling set, with 28 four-by-eight mirror and neon panels capable of vertical and rotating movements. This allows different ceiling heights and configurations ranging from complete enclosure to sloped, pitched or staggered volumes. The "Bumper Room," furnished solely in four-inch thick black vinyl tubing and a tilted, mirrored back wall that reflects suspended motorcycle lights is a place to "get away" while remaining involved. A computer controlled, two-speed bridge moves over the dancers' heads between the back-stage and the proscenium. Complete with airport runway lights and fog-smoke machines, it can carry up to 250 people. The Mezzanine's original seats were removed and replaced with carpeting and bolsters. This area affords the "best seats in the house," with spectacular views of the DJ/Media booth and the 10,000 potential special effects.

CLIENT: Studio 54 DESIGN TEAM: R. Scott Bromley, Jerry Caldari, Robert Currie, Brian Thompson DESIGN FIRM: Bromley Caldari Architects PC
SQUARE FOOTAGE: N/A BUDGET: N/A PHOTOGRAPHER: Jaime Ardiles-Arce

TEMPEST

Houston, Texas

"The Tempest is about a mystical, transforming storm," says Jordan Mozer of Shakespeare's last play; it is this same storm that seems to swirl through Mozer's latest effort, the Houston restaurant and dance club Tempest. All of the design elements, from the twisted, glowing box lamps to the swooping maple bars suggest movement and change. The eye of this tumultuous atmosphere is the central chandelier, fashioned of copper and etched blown glass, which has spines formed into a whirlpool pattern. A *tempietto*, a popular Italian architectural conceit of Shakespeare's time, whose lower sections are clad in the same black fabric as the custom chairs, is warped as if buckling in a gale. The ceiling lamps it shelters, smaller versions of the chandelier, have spines pointing toward a common direction, lending them a windblown aspect.

The theme of magical transformation that runs through Shakespeare's play is also prevelant in Tempest. Mosaic renditions of symbols representing love and luck can be found between the radii extending from the club's center. A mural filled with pictures drawn from Prospero's notebooks covers the wall behind the bar. The shelving is twisted grotesquely, suggesting a state of total flux.

© Chas McGrath

© Chas McGrath

CLIENT: N/A   DESIGN TEAM: Jordan Mozer   DESIGN FIRM: Jordan Mozer & Associates, Limited   SQUARE FOOTAGE: 4,500   BUDGET: $562,500   PHOTOGRAPHER: Chas McGrath

THE CATWALK
Kowloon, Hong Kong

The overall design concept in remodeling this former penthouse within a 12-year-old building was to create something timeless, with an air of finery and sophistication, but not a space that would be cold and austere; it had to be inviting, comfortable and fun. The result was its transformation into the Catwalk split-level night spot.

Upon entering the Catwalk, one is greeted by the reception area, with its exotic, faux animal skin carpeting, and paw-printed reception desk. This theme, along with the giant, wall-mounted, red aluminum scrolls of "wrapping paper" continue in the interior, main bar area. This space also contains the stairway to the catwalk, upstairs karaoke bar and private VIP karaoke rooms. The stainless steel banister enhances the clean-lined sophisticated decor. The live entertainment room's look, with its "horned" chandeliers is reminiscent of midwestern design, while the karaoke rooms bestow a feeling of classic comfort in the designers' careful selections of seating materials and color scheme.

CLIENT: New World Hotel DESIGN TEAM: Robert J. DiLeonardo, President; Christopher Cooney, Project Manager; Robert Bliss, Project Architect; Tom Limone, Project Designer; Nancy Spirito, Project Specifier DESIGN FIRM: DiLeonardo International, Inc. SQUARE FOOTAGE: 5,500 BUDGET: $120,000,000 (Hong Kong Dollars) PHOTOGRAPHERS: Josie Desrochers, Arthur Kan Photography

Arthur Kan Photography

Arthur Kan Photography

THE TUNNEL

New York, New York

For Tunnel, the largest night club in New York City, Robert Singer wanted to implement different lighting designs based on the concept of each individual space while retaining a cohesive overall design. It is the juxtaposition between the industrial and the opulent that gives power to the look of the interior and creates exciting visual effects. Exposed brick and industrial I-beams on the lower level stand out sharply against classical murals, sculptures, and the elegant light fixtures. Lighting is used for effect, elevating the drama of the space, rather than for task. For example the arch shape tunnel, accented by a xenon projector that simulates a laser tunnel effect.

The Tunnel is also unique in that it was the first club to use crystal chandeliers with special effects. These lights can move in and out of the area over the dance floor, either opening up the space or creating a more intimate, dining room feel.

Robert Singer Photographer

CLIENT: Eli Dayan DESIGN TEAM: Robert Singer, Lighting Designer; Marino & Associates, Architects DESIGN FIRM: Marino & Associates SQUARE FOOTAGE: 12,000 BUDGET: $2.5 million PHOTOGRAPHER: Robert Singer and John Letourneau Photography

Robert Singer Photographer

UNION

Chicago, Illinois

Union is a progressive, internationally award winning, up-scale night club cited for exemplary environmental design. Union utilizes a unique mix of materials, finishes and lighting that create an engaging, textural space while maintaining an intimate, residential feeling. Lighting is soft but dramatic and plays off a variety of patterned metal work. Exposed brick walls, faced with black leather banquettes, serve as an interesting backdrop to strategically placed lighting, video monitors and artwork. The Pool area is decorated with unusual sculpture in the shape of huge billiards balls both hung from and set into the ceiling and walls. The Union is an example of creative design transformed into a night club with a highly appealing ambiance.

CLIENT: **Facade Ltd.** DESIGN TEAM: **James Geer, President; Larry Brown, Design Associate** DESIGN FIRM: **555 Design Fabrication Mgmt., Inc.**
SQUARE FOOTAGE: **3,300** BUDGET: **$350,000** PHOTOGRAPHER: **555 Design**

555 Design

555 Design

Taverns and Bars

CAFE IGUANA
New York, New York

Robert Singer, for his lighting design for Cafe Iguana, envisioned a lizard in a Mexican courtyard enjoying the setting sun, "…the sun's last rays casting colors and shadow throughout the space." This "Mexican sunset" look was created by backlighting wood slatting in the bar and dining areas and by washing the ceiling in a golden amber color streaked with flame and sky blue. Adding to this Mexican ambiance are the mural of the desert in bloom, the vines that hang from the ceiling and the wicker seating. The centerpiece of this fun and unusual cafe is, of course, the fourteen foot long iguana fashioned from an aircraft aluminum frame reinforced by fiberglass and polyadam concrete and draped with strings of Italian crystal. Hung diagonally over the bar, this light sculpture adds a sense of intimacy and warmth to the high-ceilinged space. A flood lamp inside its head is aimed through the crystals in the eyes and gives an "aurora borealis" effect to the crystal pendants on the edge-lit crown. Presiding regally over the cafe, the "iguana" reflects and diffracts the light of eight spots, and when the nearby HVAC fans are on, ripples and sparkles in the breeze.

CLIENT: **Jerry Shaloal** DESIGN TEAM: **Robert Singer, Lighting Design; Larry Bogdanow, Architect** DESIGN FIRM: **Larry Bogdanow & Associates, Inc., Architecture; Robert Singer Assoc., Inc., Lighting Design** SQUARE FOOTAGE: **8,000** BUDGET: **$1.5 million** PHOTOGRAPHER: **Robert Singer and John Letourneau Photography**

MARITA'S CANTINA
Springfield, Pennsylvania

Because this restaurant was located in a not-too-heavily trafficked mall, next to a parking lot which was virtually empty at night, an exciting, almost forbidding environment that would be highly attractive to a young market looking for fun and excitement was desired by the client.

The restaurant which previously existed in this space had a layout in which the bar was the focal point. Sleek lines and subdued colors at the bar area now draw attention away from it, directing it instead toward the uninhibited, Mexican-inspired wall murals and the mini art gallery directly above the bar. Dramatic lighting, including the cluster lights hanging from the ceiling, highlights the intricate patterns featured there. The choice of colors and furnishings in this space combine to establish its exotic and electrifying mood.

Mark Ballogg, Steinkamp/Ballogg, Chicago

CLIENT: **Tushar Mody/Marita's of Haverford** DESIGN TEAM: **Marve H. Cooper, Principal/Designer; James Boley, Architect** DESIGN FIRM: **Marve Cooper Design** SQUARE FOOTAGE: **3,200** BUDGET: **$75,000** PHOTOGRAPHY: **Mark Ballogg, Steinkamp/Ballogg, Chicago**

MERCHANT'S

New York, New York

Exuding warmth and grace, Merchant's restaurant and bar in Manhattan is a space that has been elegantly divided into three sections: a high-ceilinged bar, an elevated dining area and a "living room." In this latter space, a homelike atmosphere is created by a working fireplace, upholstered furnishings and earth-toned colors. Brass torchieres provide accent lighting to further promote an atmosphere of coziness and comfort. A chair rail is established to create architectural interest, and a small stencil flanks the room at the ceiling line to detract the viewer's attention from duct work and architectural support elements.

The dining area, cordoned by an all-wood balcony rail features a copper mesh ceiling and mica window shutters. Upward facing track lighting and translucent, box-shaped sconces give the room a lustrous glow. The bar area features a large half-oval mirror and an abundance of dark wood grains. The richly stained ceiling beams conceal pipes, ducts, lighting and the acoustical insulation which is necessary due to residential tenants directly above the bar/restaurant.

CLIENT: Abraham Merchant, Andy Emmet DESIGN TEAM: Larry Bogdanow, Principal; Warren Ashworth, Associate; Randi Halpern, Interior Designer DESIGN FIRM: L. Bogdanow & Associates, Architects SQUARE FOOTAGE: 2,000 BUDGET: $185,000 PHOTOGRAPHER: Ross Muir

PLANET HOLLYWOOD
South Coast Plaza
Santa Ana, California

Inspired by the glamour of its namesake, Planet Hollywood is a fast-paced, exciting eatery that is set into an urban shopping center. A dramatic porte-cochère extends from the opulent deco exterior, and is surrounded on its perimeter by a ribbon of movie reel. On the interior, the casual dining atmosphere is enlivened by the abundance of the latest in Hollywood memorabilia—aliens, robots and submarines giving the space a sense of the fantasy and fun Hollywood is known for. Rooms create movie sets: one the interior of a spaceship, another mimicking a hilltop setting overlooking the urban sprawl of Los Angeles. The multi-hued, glimmering lights create their own theatrical display, providing a bright and vibrant ambiance for what is truly a nightspot for the '90s

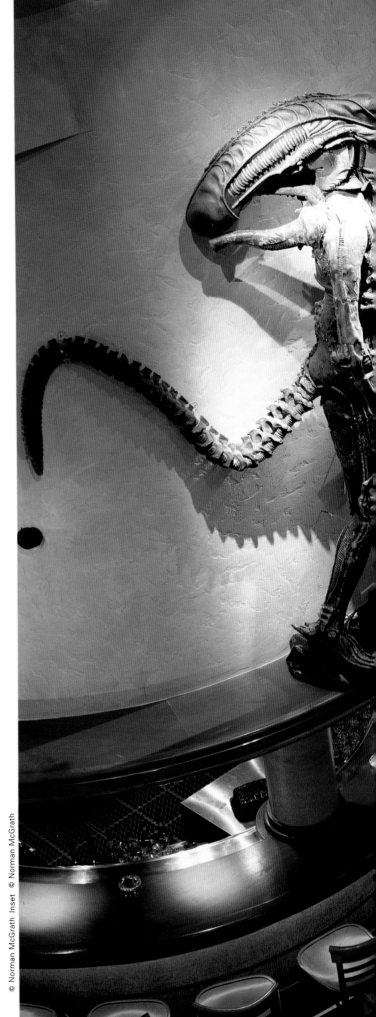

© Norman McGrath Inset © Norman McGrath

CLIENT: Italatin, Inc. DESIGN TEAM: Jeff Hatch, Jackie Hanson DESIGN FIRM: Hatch Design Group SQUARE FOOTAGE: 9,200 BUDGET: $3.2 million
PHOTOGRAPHER: © Norman McGrath

SCORES—A SPORTS BAR

New York, New York

Scores is an upscale sports bar that provides customers with fun in a participatory way. Upon entering, customers are greeted by the reception area, allowing a view into the main space, which reflects fun, movement and visual excitement in its confetti-styled carpeting and colorful, simply styled furniture. A large, 24-foot, serpentine-shaped bar, outlined in bright red, enhances the playfulness and overall exuberance of the space.

The VIP area was developed "for members only." This smaller, quieter room, was created to reflect intimacy, warmth and comfort. Here, if desired, business can be conducted with the fax, photocopying and word processing services available. To promote a "living room feeling," ceiling heights were lowered, as prevalent in private residences. Lighting levels were dimmed, warm wood finishes were used on the bar and tabletops, and colors were subdued and soft. Large-scaled tub chairs were selected for maximum comfort.

Jon Elliot/Photographer Inset: Jon Elliot/Photographer

CLIENT: Scores Entertainment, Inc. DESIGN TEAM: Robert Parnes, AIA Principal; Carol Tobin, ASID Principal; Kenn Karseboom, Project Director DESIGN FIRM: Tobin/Parnes Design Enterprises SQUARE FOOTAGE: 15,000 BUDGET: withheld at owners' request PHOTOGRAPHER: Jon Elliot

Jon Elliot/Photographer

TABLEAUX

Tokyo, Japan

Creating an environment unlike anything seen in Japan was the goal for Margaret O'Brien in her design for the Tableaux restaurant and bar in Tokyo, and it is apparent that she has succeeded beautifully. A dramatic mood is immediately created at the bar's ornate wrought iron entrace arch, which, with its stars and decorative brass crescent moon conjures a celestial theme. This celestial motif is carried throughout the bar in the design for the barstools, in the decorative stained glass window, and in the crystal-studded curtains. The ceiling also reflects the theme, having raised sections trimmed in chandelier crystal and shaped in the form of a star and quarter moon.

The dramatic setting is enhanced by a "post-apocalyptic" fresco on the bar's rear wall, cracked, mosaic-tile mirrors, and striking, hardwood mirror frames engraved with mythological characters.

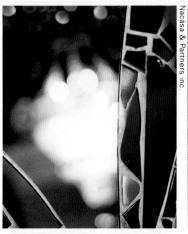

CLIENT: **Kozo Hasegawa/Hasegawa Enterprises** DESIGN TEAM: **Margaret O'Brien, Design & Architecture; Ren Makabe, Sculpture & Mural** DESIGN FIRM: **O'Brien & Associates** SQUARE FOOTAGE: **3,800** BUDGET: **$1.5 Million** PHOTOGRAPHER: **Nacása & Partners Inc.**

Nacása & Partners inc. Inset: Nacása & Partners inc.

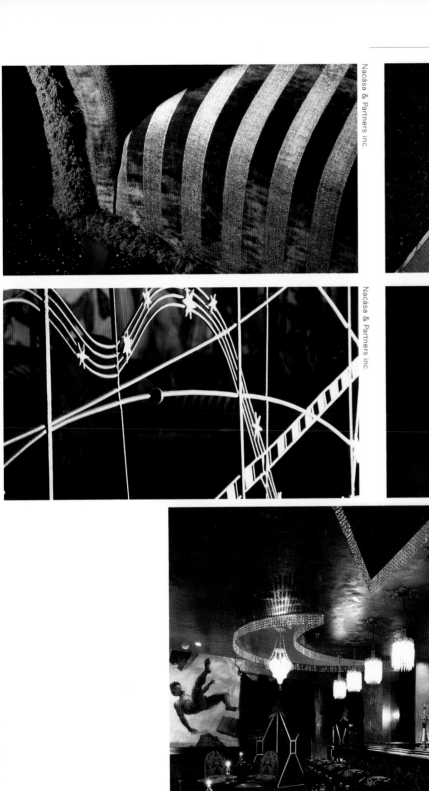

Nacása & Partners inc.

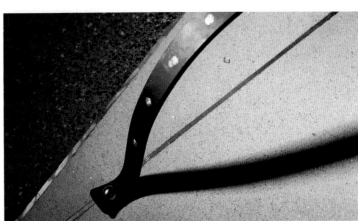

Nacása & Partners inc.

Nacása & Partners inc.

Nacása & Partners inc.

Nacása & Partners inc.

Specialty Bars

CAFFÉ NEO

Studio City, California

This urban coffeehouse was created as a small and intimate gathering place of the '90s, a replacement for the neighborhood bar. Store front windows and doors were moved to guide the patrons easily into the space where they could socially interact or pick up quick serve items without disrupting patrons in the dining area. Natural materials are combined with basic shapes and subdued colors to impart a comfortable air for informal interaction and conversation. The triangular-shaped tables create a feeling of intimacy for customers who choose to take a seat by the window. Interesting splashes of color and subdued lighting lend to the overall easy feeling of the space.

The stools and chairs are designed in geometric configurations to further continue this theme. The chairs were constructed using commonly milled sizes and supporting cross members. This created a natural juxtaposition, allowing the chairs to serve as a rudimentary ornamentation, while retaining a simple and pure form.

CLIENT: Mike Vlastas DESIGN TEAM: Gina Muzingo, Principal; Jonathon Turnbull, Principal DESIGN FIRM: Muzingo Associates SQUARE FOOTAGE: 504 BUDGET: $37,800 PHOTOGRAPHER: Ron Pollard

GORDON BIERSCH
San Francisco, California

A modern fixture of the San Franciscan waterfront at the Embarcadero, the Gordon Biersch Brewery Restaurant attracts crowds with its microbrewed lager beer and eclectic menu. The bar/restaurant, which is located in the landmark Hills Brothers Coffee building, is marked at its front entrance by a corrugated steel grain silo, and elevated, stylized signage. This silo both establishes the bar's updated and upscale image and its identity as a fully functional microbrewery. The historic rear lobby also highlights the site's functionality, with glass walls showcasing the brewery's gleaming steel vats.

The designers worked with the existing, rough textures and materials of the building in creating the interior. Exposed brick, unadorned pillars, and cut-out areas between levels (that expose bare cross-sections of concrete), present a foundation of basic materials. Onto this stark canvas were placed the rich mahogany of the bar and stools, the tomato red leather booths and the antiseptic steel of the brewing equipment.

Richard Barnes ©

NOTE: ADDITIONAL 3000 sf OF BASEMENT BREWERY NOT SHOWN

FIRST FLOOR PLAN

SECOND FLOOR PLAN

CLIENT: **Gordon Biersch Brewing Company, Inc.** DESIGN TEAM: (Allied Architects) Roddy Creedon, Partner in Charge; Scott Williams, Partner; Lorin Hill, Project Manager; Douglas Bumham, Jane Chun, Tim Contreras, Grog Ensslen, Karen Mar, Neil O'Shea, Gabriel Smith (Interim Office of Architecture) Bruce Tomb, Partner in Charge; John Randolph, Partner; Vanessa Belli, Anthony Cava DESIGN FIRM: **Allied Architects, in association with Interim Office of Architecture** SQUARE FOOTAGE: **16,000** BUDGET: **$3.2 million** PHOTOGRAPHER: Richard Barnes ©

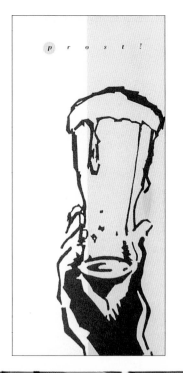

Richard Barnes © Inset: Richard Barnes ©

HONMURA AN

New York, New York

Western materials and planning are utilized with a Japanese sensitivity to design in Honmura An, a fine restaurant and bar located in downtown New York City. Bistro-style bench seats follow both long walls of the space, and a "family" table in front of the noodle booth promotes relaxed dining and drinking in the style of the traditional Japanese *Nomiya* (drinking place similar to a pub).

Traditional materials such as cherry wood, stone, custom raw steel, exposed brick and handmade papers are used to create a clean, uncluttered look. A monochromatic color scheme, warmed only by natural wood finishes, underscores this tranquil mood. Strategically located sculptures provided by the owner and his team quietly lend a sense of visual interest, while the pure, graceful lines that flow through the bar/restaurant add to the zen-like feel.

CLIENT: **Honmura An Inc.** DESIGN TEAM: **Richard Bloch, Architect, Principal; Frank Kugler, Architect** DESIGN FIRM: **Richard Bloch Architect** SQUARE FOOTAGE: **1,870** BUDGET: **$450,000** PHOTOGRAPHER: **Tom Reiss**

Tom Reiss Inset: Tom Reiss

NEWSBAR
New York, New York

Newsbar, located in Manhattan's Flatiron District, is a combination espresso bar and upscale newsstand. Its location is strategic—on 19th Street and Fifth Avenue—the center of a rapidly growing design population. It is a place where one can choose from a variety of magazines and newspapers; espresso and *lattes*; and herbal teas and breakfast/lunch specials.

Designed in a linear, monochromatic style, Newsbar is both information intensive and minimalist in decor. Reminiscent of the corner luncheonette, it is furnished with satellite tables and seats that revolve around steel bases. In a bow to clean-lined modernity, ceiling-mounted television sets and black clocks punctuate the stark white walls. Enhancing the modern mood of Newsbar are the galvanized metal racks along one wall which hold the various periodicals, flat racks at the bottom that hold newspapers, and the espresso bar which is an amalgam of concrete, metal and translucent fiberglass. The contemporary interior serves as a direct contrast to the early 1900s exterior facade of the building.

CLIENT: Leighton's News Corporation DESIGN TEAM: Wayne Turett, AIA, Designer; Bruce Garmendia, Project Manager; Lester Evan Tour, Noreen Williams DESIGN FIRM: Turett Collaborative Architects SQUARE FOOTAGE: 650 (sales floor) 750 (cellar) BUDGET: $153,000 PHOTOGRAPHER: © Paul Warchol, Paul Warchol Photography

PASQUA COFFEE BAR
Civic Center Plaza
Los Angeles, California

The Los Angeles Civic Center site is a city block-sized park/plaza in which the first free-standing, exterior Pasqua location was constructed. The building site was formerly a raised planter box over the roof of a parking garage, and the building's current slab now spans what were the planter walls. Steel framing simultaneously provides a "thin" structure, while conforming to codes requiring seismic resistance. Careful attention was given to roofing materials and details due to the structure's position beneath several mid-rise office buildings, while extensive glass areas make this greenhouse-style coffee bar's interior highly visible to plaza pedestrians.

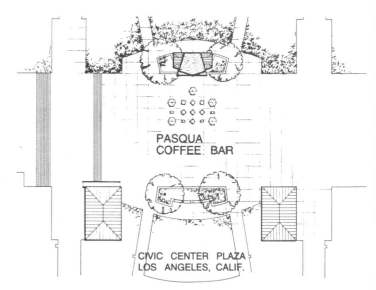

CLIENT: **Pasqua, Inc.** DESIGN TEAM: **Stephen Elbert, Architect, Principal; Elizabeth Nedell, Associate, Design and Production** DESIGN FIRM: **Elbert Associates** SQUARE FOOTAGE: **625** BUDGET: **$235,000** PHOTOGRAPHER: ©1992 Sandra Williams

PASQUA COFFEE BAR
Hope St.
Los Angeles, California

A four story glass atrium, with window walls and a sloping roof provides a dramatic and highly visible setting for this location's free-standing kiosk. Pasqua wanted to establish a strong, iconographic image in this corporate setting while blending as many of the atrium's materials and details as possible into the design. Both the kiosk's granite base and the edges and materials of the angular food preparation area match other existing constructions while the kiosk's triangular shape challenges the rectangular volumes of the atrium. Both the signature Pasqua "polished-copper," and the logo and menu boards that are set off against a black metal grid that screens food preparation areas firmly establish an individual identity in this corporate setting.

© 1992 Sandra Williams Inset: © 1992 Sandra Williams

CLIENT: **Pasqua, Inc.** DESIGN TEAM: **Stephen Elbert, Architect, Principal; Elizabeth Nedell, Associate, Design and Production; Sahoko Tamagawa, Model Maker** DESIGN FIRM: **Elbert Associates** SQUARE FOOTAGE: **250** BUDGET: **$90,000** PHOTOGRAPHER: © 1992 Sandra Williams

PASQUA COFFEE BAR Pine St.

San Francisco, California

Although not the smallest of the Pasqua locations, this tall corner site in San Francisco affords very little frontage. The equipment relationships were carefully organized, therefore, to maximize free space, while Pasqua's signature "polished-copper" surfaces create an illusion of openness. Interior walls layered in bright colors and exciting surface textures elevate the bar's mood and produce a sense of visual excitement.

CLIENT: Pasqua, Inc. DESIGN TEAM: Stephen Elbert, Architect, Principal; Elizabeth Nedell, Associate, Design and Production DESIGN FIRM: Elbert Associates SQUARE FOOTAGE: 326 BUDGET: $46,000 PHOTOGRAPHER: Eric Sahlin

PINUCCIO

Highland Park, Illinois

Slick, hip and inviting, Pinuccio is a capuccino and gelato bar that evokes strong images of Italy without utilizing more obvious Italian components. The North Chicago suburb bar abounds with excellent design, but one's eye is immediately drawn to the floor-to-ceiling triads of black metal legs on which the tables are raised and lowered. This cool, high-tech touch is more than balanced by the warmth of both the varicolored, canted side wall which has been painted, glazed and waxed to suggest a deep Mediterranean blue and the ancient-looking rear wall which has been layered with ocher paint, plaster and faded frescoes. Niches have also been set into the side wall, in which an ever-changing assortment of paintings, which are for sale, are displayed. Other Italian touches include the black and white striping, which was designed specifically to recall the facades of Renaissance churches in Italy, and the service counter, which is shaped in the form of the Italian icon, the vault.

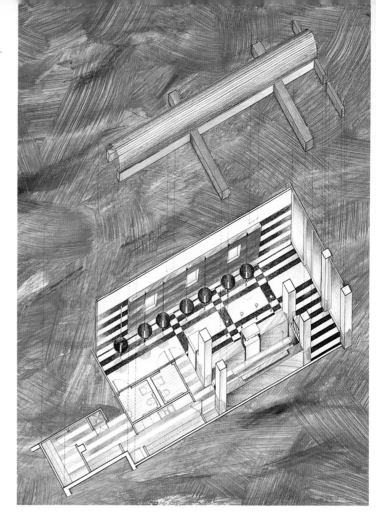

CLIENT: **PINUCCIO** Capuccino and Gelato Bar DESIGN TEAM: Dario Tainer, Principal; Andrew Groeger, Adrienne Brodin, Peter Juergens, Kurt Williams; Clark Ellithorpe, Murals DESIGN FIRM: **Tainer Associates Ltd.** SQUARE FOOTAGE: **1,200** BUDGET: **$66,000** PHOTOGRAPHER: Francois Robert

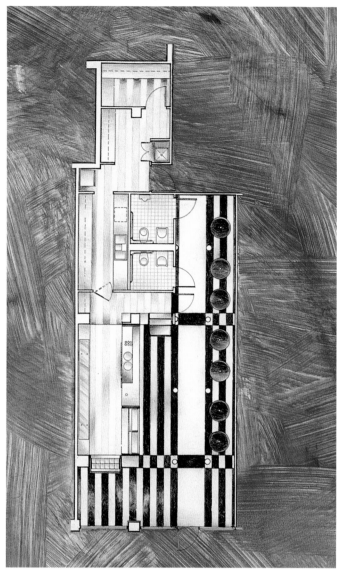

ROCKY AOKI
New York, New York

This sushi bar was built as part of the Studio 54 nightspot. To provide drama and to emphasize its location at the top of the club, lighting emphasizes the elaborate plaster molding on the ceiling. A plexiglass sign with red neon letters announces that you have reached Rocky Aoki's Sushi Palace. Black lacquer chairs surrounding stainless steel tables and a room divider of translucent glass backlit with blue neon and topped with steel pyramid capitals gives the space a high tech, very Japanese look.

CLIENT: Benihana National   DESIGN TEAM: David Rockwell; Jay Haverson
DESIGN FIRM: Haverson/Rockwell Architects P.C.   SQUARE FOOTAGE: 2,500
BUDGET: $175,000   PHOTOGRAPHER: © 1993 Mark Ross

© 1993 Mark Ross   Inset: © 1993 Mark Ross

Bars within Hotels and Restaurants

BOCCE

Minneapolis, Minnesota

Located across the street from the Target Center, home to the NBA Timberwolves, Bocce was designed to create an interior fashioned after the masculine theme of a "contemporary sporting club" while at the same time stylish enough to be a desirable space for women. The exotic zebra, caribou and wild boar trophies, leopard printed horse hides and vintage prints depicting a variety of international sports activities provide a sporting flavor, while contemporary Italian and customized furnishings and lighting add an updated atmosphere.

Bocce's second level serves as the main entry and is the focal point of the interior. It leads to a building sculpture of trapezoid staircases and suspended bridges that is designed to transport guests throughout the facility, and to create a "see and be seen" atmosphere. There is also a pivotal, connective atrium which spans all of the club's levels.

Against the backdrop of the building's exposed beamed ceilings and brick paver floors, a bold palette of black, tomato red, dill green and mustard is introduced. Emphasis is placed on the integration of the colors through the use of painted surfaces and padded wall panels.

CLIENT: **D'amico + Partners** DESIGN TEAM: **Richard D'amico, President; Gerri Summerville, Design Associate** DESIGN FIRM: **D'amico + Partners** SQUARE FOOTAGE: **8,900** BUDGET: **$1.2 Million** PHOTOGRAPHER: **Tom Berthiaume/Parallel Productions**

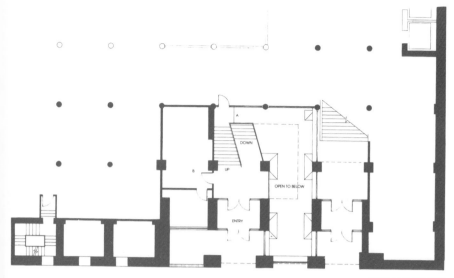

STREET LEVEL ENTRANCE

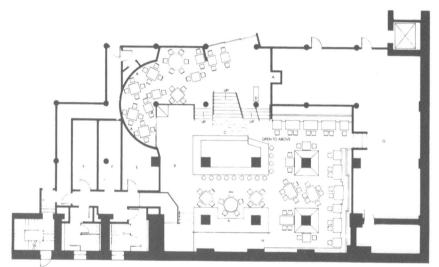

FIRST FLOOR

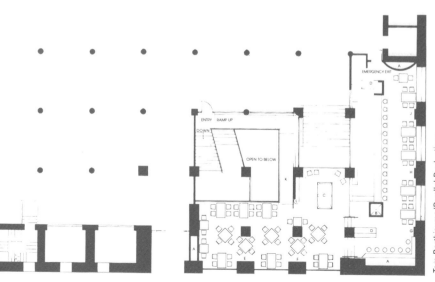

SECOND FLOOR

Tom Berthiaume/Parallel Productions

BOLIDO

New York, New York

Bolido, located in the Chelsea section of New York City, follows a futuristic motif influenced by Massimo Iosa-Ghini's background in set design and comic book illustration. Sweeping curves flow throughout the nightspot, from the curving entranceway, to the graceful tubing supporting the chairs and barstools to the focal-point stairway that connects the club's two levels. The undulating bar, lit by a complimentary soffit, enhances this ultramodern interior. The use of stainless steel tubing in the railings, the seating and the table supports retains a clean uncluttered look. Offsetting the almost antiseptic feel of these design elements are the murals and paintings that surround the club. Reminiscent of the work of the futurist movement of early twentieth-century Italy, the art was conceptualized by Iosa-Ghini and rendered in Italy. Also of Italian origin are the large entry sculpture and the custom, leather-covered banquette seating on the ground and mezzanine levels.

CLIENT: Gian Carlo Soresina DESIGN TEAM: Robert Singer, Lighting Designer DESIGN FIRM: Robert Singer & Assoc., Inc. SQUARE FOOTAGE: 8,500 BUDGET: N/A PHOTOGRAPHER: Robert Singer

Robert Singer Photographer

Robert Singer Photographer

Robert Singer Photographer

CAFE JAPONAIS

New York, New York

Cafe Japonais, which serves a mixture of French and Japanese cuisine, offers a striking visual appeal which is far from traditional. Logo signage in the front display window combines the French influence of Toulouse-Lautrec with streamers that recall the tails of Japanese kites. The bright, vivid hues Toulouse-Lautrec favored dominate the restaurant, including turquoise wall glazing (which gives an underwater feel,) and an all-around light trough with lavender gels. These bright hues are reflected by the metallic ceiling (retained by the owner) and the back mirroring of the elevated sushi counter. Angular banquettes parallel the form of the cocktail bar. Zig-zag soffits are decorated with murals designed by Lynn Matsuoka, whose sushi-chef husband was a *sumo* wrestler. They depict wrestlers in traditional, ceremonial rituals, and a few updated scenes such as a sleeping, Walkman wearing wrestler.

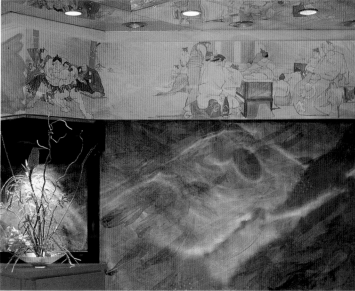

CLIENT: **Howard Stein** DESIGN TEAM: **Samuel Botero, Principal** DESIGN FIRM: **Samuel Botero Assoc., Inc.** SQUARE FOOTAGE: **2,500** BUDGET: **$400,000** PHOTOGRAPHER: **Phillip H. Ennis Photography**

Phillip H. Ennis

Phillip H. Ennis

CHARLEY'S CRAB

Fort Lauderdale, Florida

Charley's Crab, in Fort Lauderdale, Florida is a bar and restaurant constructed in a building that was in extremely poor mechanical and physical condition. By gutting the interior and removing much of the exterior walls, a single "design" idea for the entire site was able to be implemented. A series of open, connecting levels, with a variety of ceiling conditions fall away to spectacular southern and western views of the intracoastal waterway.

Large raw and beverage bars are located at the restaurant's entrance on the top level, and afford comfortable gathering and waiting areas. Twenty percent of the project's budget was used for the custom mahogany and stainless steel details. These produce a "yachting" ambiance without the use of typical "seafaring" artifacts. Light pastel-colored fabric drapes the main ceiling to break up its almost oppressive mass and to gently mimic the water surround. Large, heavy wing chairs on casters complete the sense of great comfort and luxury for this fine dining seafood restaurant.

CLIENT: **C.A. Muer Corp.** DESIGN TEAM: **Richard Bloch, Principal Design Architect** DESIGN FIRM: **Richard Bloch Architect** SQUARE FOOTAGE: **12,000** BUDGET: **$1 million** PHOTOGRAPHER: **Tom Reiss**

EMBASSY SUITES HOTEL
Various Bar Areas
New York, New York

"**B**y embracing the unique elements of this site, the building is one where form is integrated with culture, providing an exciting and spirited experience for pedestrians, theater-goers, and hotel guests" says partner Bruce Fowle of this unique hotel that contains a restaurant, three bars, and various other hotel function areas, including dining, meeting and conference rooms.

The exciting interior bar areas invite hotel guests as well as other local patrons to enter and experience the vitality that New York City has to offer. Skylights, combined with overhead scaffolding and lighting bring elegance into the double-height piano bar. The entrance to a separate bar, known as the Sky Bar, or Complimentary Bar, is marked by its tall, overhead trusses, painted bright red, and set off by the dark carpeting, which emphasizes the size and openness of the space. The design scheme imbues the rooms with a classic, elegant ambiance.

Photo by: Peter Paige

CLIENT: Silverstein Properties and General Electric Pension Fund DESIGN TEAM: Robert F. Fox, Jr., AIA; Bruce S. Fowle, FAIA; Martha A. Burns DESIGN FIRM: Fox & Fowle Architects SQUARE FOOTAGE: 430,000 (Hotel) BUDGET: witheld at owners' request PHOTOGRAPHER: Peter Paige

Photo by : Peter Paige

Photo by : Peter Paige

EMPIRE CLUB
Radisson Empire Hotel
New York, New York

The Radisson Empire has stood solidly at 63rd and Broadway since 1924. It has recently undergone renovation at the hands of Tom Lee Ltd., and has become a place of dazzling interest and excitement. The talent and intrigue of Lincoln Center, located just across the street, have been brought into the hotel, visible in its varied interior design schemes and murals.

One of the highlights of the Radisson is its Empire Club; a wonderful clubby lounge with an antique billiards table, Edwardian Bar, chess boards and backgammon games. The late nineteenth century portrait above the bar sets the tone for this Old English-style room. Dark wood, leather and understated patterns give the space an antique and masculine, yet comfortable and relaxed ambiance.

Photo by: Peter Paige   Inset: Photo by: Peter Paige

CLIENT: **John Kluge** DESIGN TEAM: **Emery Roth**, Project Architect; **Gran Sultan**, Field Architect DESIGN FIRM: **Tom Lee Ltd.** SQUARE FOOTAGE: **1,330** BUDGET: **witheld at owners' request** PHOTOGRAPHER: **Peter Paige**

GRAND HYATT WAILEA

Maui, Hawaii

Moody and dramatic, the disco of the Grand Hyatt Wailea is a space designed to be completely different from the rest of the hotel. Strong contrasts dominate the club. Bright, energetic colors give visual impact even in darker areas of the space. Monolithic concrete columns are set with elegant, gilt sconces while thick carpeting is used in the side seating areas (as opposed to the bare flooring of the bar and dance areas) to retain intimate space within the club.

Large, edge-lit circular recesses set into the ceiling give off a soft luminescence, while spot and technical lighting creates excitement in the dance area. The fluorescent neon, used overhead in the corridor spanning the disco, is formed in irregular rippling patterns that give the space an enticing, aquatic ambiance.

Jaime Ardiles-Arce

CLIENT: Hideki Hayashi, TSA International, Ltd. DESIGN TEAM: Robert E. Barry, Designer; Danny Laureano & Bernie Miranda, Project Managers; Charles Lee, Project Coordinator; Alisa Chodos, Project Manager in Charge of Decoration DESIGN FIRM: Barry Design Associates SQUARE FOOTAGE: 9,300 BUDGET: $640 million (hotel) PHOTOGRAPHER: Jaime Ardiles-Arce

JANOS
Tucson, Arizona

This restaurant, once the home of Hiram Stevens, and before that, Marshall Duffield, was built between 1859 and 1864, for Stevens' new wife, Petra Santa Cruz. It is one of Tucson's oldest family homes and the site of much local history. At Janos, great pleasure is taken in telling the stories of that fascinating era of American history, as well as in giving guests a tour of this historical place.

Upon entering the restaurant, the *maitresse d'hotel* greets you with a tour of the house, revealing the elegant rooms with their thick adobe walls, plain wooden floors and fourteen-foot ribbed ceilings made of dried saguaro beams. There is an array of cozy dining spaces, each individually designed, with original, local art hung on the old walls. The feeling of antiquity is further enhanced at the bar area, with its countertop of galvanized steel, ornate, antique barstools, and plethora of wood, which appears to have weathered many generations of celebration.

William Lesch

CLIENT: **Janos and Rebecca Wilder** DESIGN TEAM: **Rory McCarthy, Project Designer** DESIGN FIRM: **Rory McCarthy Design** SQUARE FOOTAGE: **2,400** BUDGET: **$200,000** PHOTOGRAPHER: **William Lesch**

LE BAR BAT

New York, New York

Transforming a once ecclesiastical space into a profane confluence of exotic ideas and images, the team of Jay Haverson and David Rockwell transformed this New York site into a Pan-asian style restaurant/club unlike anything seen before. Such wide-ranging influences as the movies "The World of Susie Wong" and "Mighty Joe Young," to travel brochures to images from opera and theater were used to fashion Le Bar Bat into a space that would offer a "mini vacation" from the pressures of urban life. This mixing of design is begun on the ground floor, where three different antique fabrics upholster the booth seating, the floor is finished in multicolored African slate and the walls are graced with five collaged wallpapers from the thirties and forties. Angled, tree-like columns engraved with oriental incscriptions cradle the central mezzanine, creating a "treehouse" effect. This is augmented by the eighteen bats that circle above. Made of handblown cobalt blue glass and copper mesh, they are internally lit and give off a magical glow.

Pandora's Box, a private club downstairs is draped in rich blue swags of crushed velour and lit by the multicolored paper lanterns that hang from the bamboo-mesh ceiling, suggesting an exotic soiree in the forests of Asia. Upstairs, the secluded Borneo room is a chandelier lit, tea-colored bar lounge that uses game boards such as chinese checkers and mah jong as tables.

CLIENT: **Joyce Steins** DESIGN TEAM: **Jay M. Haverson & David S Rockwell,** **Partners; Carmen Agular, Project Manager; James Am, Design Assistant** DESIGN FIRM: **Haverson/Rockwell Architects P.C.** SQUARE FOOTAGE: **14,500** BUDGET: **$2 million** PHOTOGRAPHER: **© Paul Warchol, Paul Warchol** **Photography**

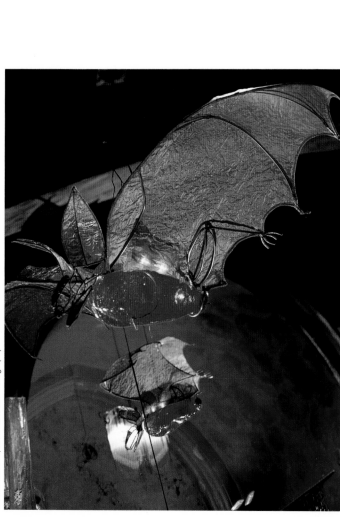

NACHO MAMMA'S

Des Moines, Iowa

Located in a space previously occupied by another Mexican bar and restaurant, and wishing to disassociate itself from the unsuccessful reputation of the former establishment, a new, "hot" visual identity was desired, therefore a lively color palette, with animated graphic designs was used. This concept is visible in the canvas awnings outside the restaurant.

In order to highlight the colorful decor, a simple black laminated countertop, combined with light wood bar stools and floor were used. To continue the excitement of the color palette indoors, a large jalapeño pepper, constructed by the Drake University chapter of Sigma Chi fraternity, was added to the bar atrium, as was the freeform graphic serpent on the far wall of the bar area.

CLIENT: Rich Murillo DESIGN TEAM: John Sayles, Designer DESIGN FIRM: Sayles Graphic Design SQUARE FOOTAGE: 9,000 BUDGET: withheld at owners' request PHOTOGRAPHER: Bill Nellans/Deer Valley Studios

ORSINI'S

New York, New York

Designed around the central concept of a refined and gracious Italian farmhouse of the 19th century, Orsini's, moved and completely redesigned after thirty years is both elegant and comfortable without reflecting the "stiff" demeanor of the site's previous occupant. Having to work around elements which were retained by the owners, including the circa 1910 painted ceiling, the mosaics decorating the vestibule walls (now protected by boarding covered with textured stucco,) and a collection of antique furniture and objets d'art, Samuel Botero managed to produce an interior that is both engaging and delightful.

Added to the existing structure was a cloak room with terrazzo flooring and an eighteenth century Tuscan commode, and the bar, backed with a trompe l'oeil finish. A residential flavor is introduced in the dining area by the use of fabric upholstering on the walls, *faux bois* windows and coffers, extensive stucco, and banquettes (some of which were retained from the previous restaurant). This feeling is enhanced by the custom lighting, which includes antique Italian sconces with pink-tinged bulbs, and filtered, low voltage halogen spots. A demi-lune of painted clouds tops the extended dining space that was closed off for private parties. Travertine flooring was left uncovered in order to add acoustic punch to the space that would otherwise have been overly muted.

CLIENT: **Armando & Elio Orsini** DESIGN TEAM: **Samuel Botero, Principal**
DESIGN FIRM: **Samuel Botero Assoc., Inc.** SQUARE FOOTAGE: **2,500** BUDGET:
$1 million PHOTOGRAPHER: **Phillip H. Ennis Photography**

Phillip H. Ennis Inset: Phillip H. Ennis

PAINTED DESERT

New York, New York

An enchanting and graceful sense of the Belle Epoque period abounds in Painted Desert, a restaurant/bar located in central Manhattan. Large Doric columns support a ceiling with wedding cake plaster moldings. Pink and white shades elevate the mood of this two-story space and add to its apparent size. A large chandelier finished dramatically in crystal provides ambient lighting. Custom wall sconces and track lighting fixtures augment the general illumination. Brass railings and an exciting zig-zagging half wall cordon the second level. A baby grand piano, perched on a platform between the two levels serves as a focal point for the room. Huge palladian windows with minimal window treatments fill the restaurant cum bar's front wall, allowing the dining patrons to be seen from the street, and adding a bright, airy feel to this delightful and extravagant space.

CLIENT: **Robert Farley** DESIGN TEAM: **Robert Farley, Interior Design; Robert Singer, Lighting Design** DESIGN FIRM: **Robert Singer & Assoc., Inc.** SQUARE FOOTAGE: **5,000** BUDGET: **N/A** PHOTOGRAPHER: **Robert Singer**

PAOLO'S
San Jose, California

Paolo's is a restaurant which manages to recreate the warmth, charm and flavor of old Tuscany within the ground floor of a contemporary high rise office complex in downtown San Jose. An inviting atmosphere is created by the use of a palette of mustard, eggplant, and olive which flows through warmly textured fabrics and carpets. Custom designed, burnished iron hand rails undulate throughout the restaurant, adding a whimsical touch. Oversized cornice beams and primitively textured walls are juxtaposed with loosely wrapped plum, gold and olive taffeta window dressings that scallop across the view. The "new-classic," European-style bar in verde patina and gloss black lends updated elegance to an otherwise traditional setting.

CLIENT: Jenny Griesbach/Carolyn Allen DESIGN TEAM: Bethe Cohen, Interior Designer; Vivian Soliemani/Ushana, Interior Designer; Jennifer Padua, Interior Designer DESIGN FIRM: Bethe Cohen Design Associates SQUARE FOOTAGE: 8,700 BUDGET: $2,001,000 PHOTOGRAPHER: Beatriz Coll, Coll Photography

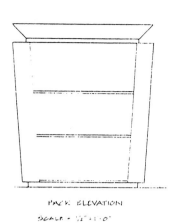

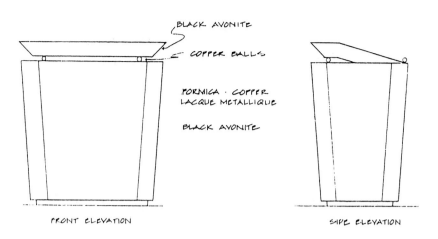

BLACK AVONITE

COPPER BALLS

FORMICA · COPPER
LACQUE METALLIQUE

BLACK AVONITE

BACK ELEVATION

SCALE = 1/2" = 1'-0"

FRONT ELEVATION

SIDE ELEVATION

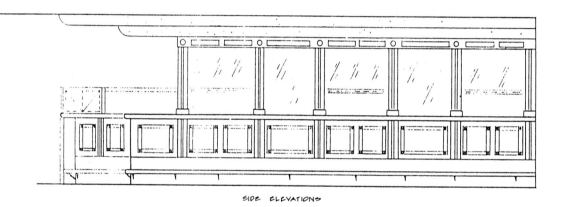

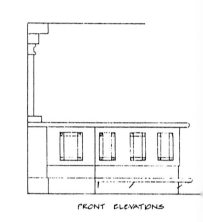

SIDE ELEVATIONS

FRONT ELEVATIONS

PRIMA DONNA
New York, New York

New York's Prima Donna offers a noisy, fun atmosphere in a setting designed to resemble a Pompeiian ruin. The client wanted an interior that, in the words of Samuel Botero, "connoted Italian opera, which led to the idea of a set design, which, in turn, led to the idea of a Pompeiian kind of ruin." The lively acoustics of the space come from the banishment of soundproofing materials from the large, single room that houses the restaurant/bar. The Pompeiian atmosphere arises largely from the three inch-thick sheetrock, "broken" at the top and detailed with marbelized wooden crown moldings, that grace the walls. The upper part of the walls and the ceiling are painted sky-blue. Combined with structural lighting that simulates scaffolding and hickory wood chairs designed to look like trees, the look of an outdoor ruin is created. This is enhanced by the treatment of new walls and columns with the same marbelized finish used in the crown moldings. The space is completed by what Botero calls "the glass box entry that frames people inside at the front of the restaurant."

Phillip H. Ennis

CLIENT: **Howard Stein** DESIGN TEAM: **Samuel Botero, President** DESIGN FIRM: **Samual Botero Assoc. Inc.** SQUARE FOOTAGE: **3,500** BUDGET: **$1 million** PHOTOGRAPHER: **Phillip H. Ennis**

RISTORANTE MORANDI

Tokyo, Japan

As a counterpoint to the often too-technological Japanese interiors, the Ristorante Morandi, located in the exclusive Ginza section of Tokyo, offers surprising softness, whimsy and ease. There is a decidedly residential flavor to the restaurant, with many antiques drawn from rural Pennsylvania, (the location of Bohn's country house). This is immediately apparent in the living room-like entrance lounge, with its antique-inspired, richly upholstered chairs and bronze-anodized steel bar. Custom, locally cast ram's leg bar stools add a playful touch.

The dining areas comprise two levels, the first secluded by blue chiffon draperies, the second, by gauzy curtains highlighted with a brown velvet drape. The building's facade is differentiated from others on the block by the use of turn-of-the-century detailing rendered in a sandstone-sheathed construction.

CLIENT: Creative Intelligence Associates, Japan (C.I.A.) DESIGN TEAM: Joseph Lembo, Laura Bohn, Naoko Kondo, Senior Designer, Lembo/Bohn; Mari Kida, International Liason, C.I.A.; Toshiaki Nonaka, Architect DESIGN FIRM: Lembo/Bohn Design Associates, Inc. SQUARE FOOTAGE: 3,430 BUDGET: **$1,622,390** PHOTOGRAPHER: Edward Hames

Edward Hames

Edward Hames

Edward Hames

Edward Hames

Edward Hames

Appendixes

Designers' Addresses

Adamstein & Demetriou
3247 Q Street NW
Washington, District of Columbia 20007
Tel: (202) 333-9038
Fax: (202) 333-9013

Allied Architects
118 Hawthorne Street
San Francisco, California 94103
Tel: (415) 495-2445

Barry Design Associates
11601 Wilshire Boulevard, Suite 102
Los Angeles, California 90025
Tel: (310) 478-6081

Bethe Cohen Design Associates
150 East Campbell Avenue, #102
Campbell, California 95008
Tel: (408) 379-4051
Fax: (408) 379-0672

Bromley Caldari Architects PC
242 West 27th Street
New York, New York 10001
Tel: (212) 820-4250

D'amico + Partner, Inc.
1402 First Avenue South
Minneapolis, Minnesota 55403
Tel: (612) 334-3366
Fax: (612) 874-0420

DiLeonardo International, Inc.
2350 Post Road
Warwick, Rhode Island 02886
Tel: (401) 732-2900
Fax: (401) 732-5315

Elbert Associates
363 17th Street
Suite 200
Oakland, California 94612
Tel: (510) 839-2992
Fax: (510) 839-2420

Fox & Fowle Architects
22 West 19th Street
New York, New York 10011
Tel: (212) 627-1700
Fax: (212) 463-8716

Hatch Design Group
3198 D Airport Loop Dr.
Costa Mesa, CA 92626
Tel: (714) 979-8385
Fax: (714) 979-6430

Haverson/Rockwell Architects P.C.
18 West 27th Street
New York, New York 10001
Tel: (212) 889-4182
Fax: (212) 725-2473

Hirsch/Bedner Associates
3216 Nebraska Avenue
Santa Monica, California 90404
Tel: (310) 829-9087

Hirschberg Design Group, Inc.
334 Queen St. East
Toronto, Ontario M5A 1S8
Tel: (416) 868-1210
Fax: (416) 868-6650

Jordan Mozer & Associates Ltd.
228 W. Illinois, 2nd Floor
Chicago, Illinois 60610
Tel: (312) 661-0060
Fax: (312) 661-0981

L. Bogdanow & Associates, Architects
75 Spring Street
New York, New York 10012
Tel: (212) 966-0313
Fax: (212) 941-8875

Lembo/Bohn Design Associates, Inc.
One Gansevoort Street
New York, New York, 10014
Tel: (212) 645-3636
Fax: (212) 645-3639

Mandi QuKay Design & Planning Inc.
11 South Street
Garden City, New York 11530
Tel: (718) 426-5997

Marve Cooper Design
2120 West Grand Avenue
Chicago, Illinois 60612
Tel: (312) 733-4250
Fax: (312) 733-9715

Michael David Berzak Architecture
1212 West 19th Street, Suite 1001
New York, New York 10011
Tel: (212) 243-2639
Fax: (212) 691-2409

Muzingo Associates
2288 Westwood Boulevard, Suite #210
Los Angeles, CA 90064
Tel: (310) 470-9181

ONE DESIGN CENTER, Inc.
2828 Lawndale Drive
Greensboro, North Carolina 27408
Tel: (919) 288-0134
Fax: (919) 282-7369

O'Brien & Associates
222 Washington Avenue, #12
Santa Monica, California 90403
Tel: (310) 458-9177
Fax: (310) 451-0812

Richard Bloch Architect
222 Park Avenue South
New York, New York 10003
Tel: (212) 475-5010
Fax: (212) 475-3184

Robert Singer & Associates, Inc.
175 Fifth Avenue, Suite 2356
New York, New York 10010
Tel: (212) 369-1300
Fax: (212) 369-1301

Samuel Botero Assoc., Inc.
150 East 58th Street, 23rd Floor
New York, New York 10155
Tel: (212) 935-5155
Fax: (212) 832-0714

Sayles Graphic Design
308 Eighth Street
Des Moines, Iowa 50309
Tel: (515) 243-2922
Fax: (515) 243-0212

Tainer Associates Ltd.
213 West Institute Place, Suite 301
Chicago, Illinois 60610
Tel: (312) 951-1656
Fax: (312) 951-8773

Tobin/Parnes Design Enterprises
270 Lafayette Street, Suite 302
New York, New York 10012
Tel: (212) 941-9800
Fax: (212) 941-9810

Tom Lee Limited
136 East 57th Street
New York, New York 10022
Tel: (212) 421-4433
Fax: (212) 758-9679

Totah Design, Inc.
654 N. Larchmont Boulevard
Los Angeles, CA 90004
Tel: (213) 467-2927
Fax: (213) 463-0377

Turett Collaborative Architects
45 West 18th St., 7th floor
New York, New York 10011
Tel: (212) 627-2530
Fax: (212) 627-4336

Photographers' Addresses

555 Design Fabrication Management Inc.
1238 South Ashland
Chicago, Illinois 60608
Tel: (312) 733-6777
Fax: (312) 733-3083

Jerome Adamstein
Los Angeles, California
Tel: (310) 289-8300

Jaime Ardiles-Arce
509 Madison Avenue
New York, New York 10022
Tel: (212) 688-9191

Daniel G. Bakke
Daniel Bakke Photography
4449 North Wolcott, #2A
Chicago, Illinois 60640
Tel: (312) 561-1902

Mark Ballogg
SteinKamp/Ballogg
311 North Des Plaines, #409
Chicago, Illinois 60661
(312) 902-1233
(312) 902-1701

Richard Barnes
Richard Barnes Photography
1403 Shotwell Street
San Francisco, California 94110
Tel: (415) 550-1023

Tom Berthiaume
Parallel Productions
2010 First Avenue South
Minneapolis, Minnesota 55404
Tel: (612) 874-1999
Fax: (612) 874-1998

Jerry Blow
Architectural Photography
911 Mordecai Drive
Raleigh, North Carolina 27604
Tel: (919) 834-3836

Beatriz Coll
Coll Photography
2445 Third Street, Suite No. 265
San Francisco, California 94107
Tel: (415) 863-0699
Fax: (510) 843-2461

Joseph Coscia Jr.
27 East 32nd Street
Bayonne, New Jersey 07002
Tel: (201) 437-0705

Christopher Dew
Christopher Dew Productions
95 Gloucester Street
Toronto, Ontario, Canada M4Y 1M2

Tel: (416) 964-6107
Fax: (416) 967-0863

Jon Elliot
329 West 85th Street
New York, New York 10024
Tel: (212) 362-0809

Philip H. Ennis
98 Smith Street
Freeport, New York 11520
Tel (516) 379-4273

Arthur Kan Photography
7 Cross Lane
1/F Wanchai
Hong Kong
Tel: 852-834-1908

William Lesch
426 South Otero
Tucson, Arizona 85701
Tel: (602) 622-6693

John Le Tourneau
P.O. Box 1088
New York, New York 10185
Tel: (212) 228-5293

Lars Lönninge
121 West 19th Street
New York, New York 10011
Tel: (212) 627-0100
Fax: (212) 633-8144

Chas McGrath
3735 Kansas Drive
Santa Rosa, California 95405
Tel: (707) 545-5853

Norman McGrath
164 West 79th Street
New York, New York 10024
Tel: (212) 799-6422
Fax: (212) 799-1285

Ross Muir
113 East 31st Street, #5B
New York, New York 10016
Tel: (212) 779-3395
Fax: (212) 941-8875

Nacása & Partners Inc.
3-5-5 Minami-Azabu, Minato-ku
Tokyo 106, Japan
Tel: 03-3444-2922
Fax: 03-3444-2678

Bill Nellans
Deer Valley Studios
3800 Waterworks Parkway
Des Moines, Iowa 50312
Tel: (515) 274-0406
Fax: (515) 274-3371

Peter Paige
Peter Paige Photography
269 Parkside Road
Harrington Park, New Jersey 07640
Tel: (201) 767-3150
Fax: (201) 767-9263

Ron Pollard
7692 South Ames Way
Littleton, Colorado 80123
Tel: (303) 756-1723
Fax: (303) 756-4832

Tom Reiss
649 East 14th Street, #1D
New York, New York 10009
Tel: (212) 673-1550

Francois Robert
740 North Wells
Chicago, Illinois 60610
Tel: (312) 787-0777
Fax: (312) 787-0778

Mark Ross
Mark Ross Photography, Inc.
345 East 80th Street
New York, New York 10021
Tel: (212) 744-7258
Fax: (212) 879-4573

Eric Sahlin
33 Home Place East, #A
Oakland, California 94610
Tel: (510) 465-0897

Robert Singer
Robert Singer & Associates, Inc.
175 Fifth Avenue
New York, New York 10010
Tel: (212) 369-1300
Fax: (212) 369-1301

Van Blerck Photography
95 Kirkwood Avenue
Merrick, New York 11566
Tel: (516) 546-4500

Paul Warchol
Paul Warchol Photography, Inc.
133 Mulberry Street
New York, New York, 10013
Tel: (212) 431-3461
Fax: (212) 274-1953

Sandra Williams
3536 Eugene Place
San Diego, California
Tel: (619) 283-3100
Fax: (619) 282-5421